Patrick Conlan OFM

THE MISSIONARY WORK OF
THE IRISH FRANCISCANS

VERITAS

First published 1996 by
Veritas Publications
7-8 Lower Abbey Street
Dublin 1

ISBN 1 85390 316 7

British Library Cataloguing
in Publication Data.
A catalogue record for
this book is available
from the British Library.

Maps drawn by Denis Barrett
Other drawings by Hilary Gilmore
Cover design by Bill Bolger
Printed in the Republic of Ireland by
Criterion Press Ltd, Dublin

CONTENTS

INTRODUCTION

When the followers of Saint Francis came to Ireland in 1226-30 it was on the edge of the Christian world. As the great colonial powers began to expand in the sixteenth century the Tudor monarchs treated Ireland as one of their colonies. Thus the Irish Franciscans had little opportunity to participate in the missionary movements of those years. Early in the seventeenth century there was a short rescue mission to Scotland. Individual friars based in the Irish Franciscan continental colleges worked as chaplains in many parts of the world during the eighteenth century. Father Bonaventure O'Donoghue was in Louisiana in 1718. Father James Dease died of fever in Calcutta in 1757, just a few years after Father Gabriel Nugent died in Haiti and after Father Andrew Plunkett had decided to try his luck in Peru.

These examples of individual friars trying to seek out a ministry and a living stand in contrast with attempts to work within missionary structures. The first organised Irish Franciscan mission was that to Newfoundland, which began in 1784. Since then many Irish friars have undertaken missionary work either as individuals helping other groups or in properly organised Franciscan missions in such places as Australia, China, South Africa, Zimbabwe and Latin America.

Respect for the individual is a characteristic of all Franciscan activity. Since the time when Friar James of Ireland is reputed to have accompanied Blessed Odoric of Pordenone to China in 1316-20, Irish Franciscans have worked in small groups, tending to avoid structured missionary activity. Even now there is one Irish friar ministering as part of an international Franciscan effort in Siberia. In Scotland, Newfoundland and Australia, they initially plugged gaps rather than working in an organised manner.

5

While the Irish were effective in introducing the Church, they tended to overlook implanting the Franciscan Order. As a result Newfoundland was left without a Franciscan presence and the same would have happened in Australia but for the vision of one friar. The missionaries in South Africa and Zimbabwe were slow to set up a formation system for young Franciscans but the Order is now flourishing in both countries. In the event, the Irish Franciscan province has given birth to the Province of the Holy Spirit (Australia and New Zealand). The Irish fathered the English and Bavarian Provinces and the Vice-province of Southern Africa. With a number of other entities, they helped to found the Province of Central America. The Custody of the Good Shepherd in Zimbabwe is well on the way to independence.

Individual friars continue to work in various parts of the world, such as England and the USA. Since their first missionary undertaking to Newfoundland in the 1780s, the contribution of the Irish Franciscans to the foreign missions, and the implanting of the Order, especially in this century, has been impressive. This book aims to make this contribution more accessible to the general reader.

Chapter 1

WORKING IN THE HOLY LAND

The Custody of the Holy Land is staffed by Franciscans from every corner of the world. Saint Francis went there in 1219-20 to see and experience the places where Christ had lived on earth. The Saint's followers set up a friary in Jerusalem in 1229. This belonged to the Province of the Holy Land, covering most of the eastern Mediterranean. It was later divided into custodies, including that of the Holy Land itself. In 1333 King Robert of Naples obtained permission from the Sultan of Egypt for the friars to look after the Basilica of the Holy Sepulchre and the shrines on Mount Sion and in Bethlehem. The friars' role as custodians of the shrines belonging to the Latin Church was confirmed by Clement VI in 1342. This is taken as the foundation date of the Custody of the Holy Land, which became an independent unit within the order while retaining the title of a custody. The Franciscans' role as official, permanent custodians was granted by Martin V in 1421.

The first Irish Franciscans in the Holy Land were Simon Fitzsimeon and Hugh the Illuminator, who left Ireland in 1322. They sailed from Dublin to Caernarvon, then overland to Chester and across the Chiltern Hills to London. After praying at the tomb of Saint Thomas à Becket in Canterbury, they sailed from Dover to Wissant. They went overland through Boulogne and Amiens to Paris. They travelled up the valley of the Seine and across to Châlon before going down the Saône and the Rhône to Marseilles. Going overland through Nice to Genoa, they crossed northern Italy to visit the tomb of Saint Anthony at Padua on their way to Venice. They then

7

sailed to Alexandria via Sicily and Crete. Hugh died in Cairo, but Simon reached Jerusalem nine months after leaving Ireland. Three months later he set out on the return journey. The diary of his travels became a best-seller in an age when the printed book did not exist.

An Irishman, James Brassel, was superior in Aleppo from 1647 to 1649 but belonged to a Spanish province of the Order. Fathers Bonaventure Burke, Anthony Mulvey and Bonaventure Kensly worked at the basilica of the Holy Sepulchre, in Sidon and in Aleppo, in the last quarter of the seventeenth century. Similarly, in the following century Irish Franciscans worked in Bethlehem, Damascus, Jerusalem and on the island of Cyprus.

Father Bonaventure McLaughlin went to Alexandria in 1840 but the climate affected his health and he had to leave after a year. Two Irish friars were in the Holy Land in the 1860s: Fathers Aloysius Stafford (Holy Sepulchre 1861-8) and James Anthony Mahoney (Cairo and Suez 1862-6). Father Aloysius was well-known for looking after English-speaking visitors to Jerusalem until he had a stroke and was invalided back to Ireland, where he died in 1882. Father James had to contend with an outbreak of cholera and returned to Rome a near-broken man. He recovered and later served as a missionary in New Zealand for twenty-three years. Father Joseph (Louis) Lynch was so keen to go to the Holy Land that he went in 1889 without proper permission and worked in Aleppo for three years before having to return to Ireland.

Father Augustine Holohan was the first of a series of military chaplains in Cyprus when he went there in 1884. Five years later he travelled to Sydney as a member of the first Franciscan community in Australia. Towards the end of the century two friars produced accounts of the mission in the Holy Land. Father Anthony Slattery wrote *Palestine: the*

Mission and the Missionaries, while Father Leonard Dunne's work remained unpublished due to his death.

The tradition of individual friars working for the Order in the Holy Land has continued in this century, beginning with Father Lawrence O'Neill at the Holy Sepulchre in 1900-01. He returned to the area as a Royal Navy chaplain during the First World War. Father Leo Sheehan, an army chaplain, rode into Jerusalem in 1918 with Allenby's Camel Corps, as they drove the Turks out of the Holy Land. Another army chaplain in the same theatre, Father Isidore O'Meehan, was accidentally shot dead by his batman in 1919 at Amara, on the banks of the Tigris, after four years of military service.

The best-known Irish Franciscan in the Holy Land in this century was Father Eugene Hoade, who worked there from 1929 to 1956. He initially taught in Terra Santa College, but is remembered for his work as superior at the Garden of Gethsemane where he completely renovated the shrine, and as chaplain to the Palestine police. Whatever about the truth of the stories of his manning a machine gun during Jewish attacks on Jerusalem, he was loved and honoured by the Arabs. His *Guide to the Holy Land* has gone through many editions and remains popular.

Father Francis (Tarcisius) Hand joined Father Eugene in 1947 and did a twelve-year stint in the Holy Land. Father P. J. (Athanasius) Giblin taught in Bethlehem from 1957 to 1960, before returning to this part of the world as one of the original emigrant chaplains to the Irish in London. The Irish Province's most recent missionary in the Holy Land was Brother Conrad McEvoy, who worked mainly at the Church of the Holy Sepulchre between 1983 and 1989.

From the early fourteenth century the Irish Franciscans have played their part, alongside friars from many other countries, in looking after the needs of the people, pilgrim or native, in the land of Jesus' birth.

Chapter 2

TO THE HIGHLANDS AND ISLANDS OF SCOTLAND

As the morale of the Franciscans in Ireland improved in the early seventeenth century, they were able to help their Celtic brethren in Scotland. A Scottish friar, Father John Ogilvie, (not to be confused with his Jesuit namesake), had been living in the new Irish Franciscan College at Louvain, and returned to Scotland in 1612. The next year he was joined by a Scottish brother, John Stuart, who had the vital local knowledge and knew Scots Gaelic. They were aware that most of the Scottish Lowlands had been lost to the Reformers. However, since the Protestant ministers could not speak Gaelic, many of the people in the Highlands and Islands were still Catholic, although they had not seen a priest for nearly fifty years. Brother John travelled back and forth to Louvain, where he died in 1625. He supplied fresh information about the mission and encouraged more priests to go there.

As early as 1611, Monsignor Bentivoglio, Papal Nuncio in Brussels, had suggested to Rome that the Irish Franciscans, who spoke the language and had Louvain as a base, were the obvious missionaries for the Highlands. In was expected that Propaganda Fide in Rome would provide the necessary financial support, but this did not materialise as readily as expected. Financial problems delayed the departure of Father Patrick Brady for the Highlands, and Father Edmund McCann for the Hebrides until 4 January 1619. Although Father Edmund was arrested, imprisoned for two years and banished, he returned with the next group of priests.

About twenty friars volunteered to go to Scotland, but there was little cash available. Eventually Fathers Edmund McCann, Paul O'Neill, Patrick Hegarty and Cornelius Ward, set out in 1623. In July 1624 they arrived on the island of Sanda, where they used an old church dedicated to Saint Ninian as their base. They then crossed over to Kintyre, where they were so successful that the local minister tried to capture them. They worked their way up the coast through Colonsay to Mull before splitting up. Father Paul had to retire to Ireland following persecution. Father Cornelius moved to Argyll, using his poetry to convert Campbell of Calder. He moved regularly between Scotland, Ireland, Louvain and Rome until he was captured in 1630 and confined to prison in London. Released through the good offices of the King of Poland, he went into exile on the Continent. He spent another short period in Scotland before retiring to Donegal, where he died in 1640. Fathers Edmund and Patrick worked in Scotland for about fifteen years before old age necessitated their retirement.

Severe persecution during 1626 forced the friars to rethink their approach. The abandoned Third Order friary at Bonamargy on the north coast of Antrim was taken over as a base. It was only twenty miles across the North Channel to the Isles of Scotland. Father Patrick Hegarty took up residence at Bonamargy in 1631 and did much good work. Many people sailed across the North Channel to avail of his spiritual services. He was arrested in 1641 and spent five years in prison. He died in 1647, a year after his release.

Lack of funds and the political situation forced the closure of the mission in 1637. Father Patrick Hegarty returned occasionally to Bonamargy until his death. Four missionaries were ready to resume missionary work but were prevented from travelling. Efforts to reopen the mission in 1647-8 also failed.

Two brothers, Mark and Francis McDonnell, recently ordained at Saint Isidore's Irish Franciscan College, Rome, volunteered for work in the Highlands in 1667. After a difficult journey, including shipwreck and having to beg their way overland to Newcastle, they began their pastoral work among the Gaelic-speakers of the Highlands early in 1668. Both suffered from ill-health and Father Mark died late in 1671. Father Francis was then working on the island of Uist. His health forced him to retire to Ireland in 1679.

In 1703 it was reported that there were five Irish Franciscans working in Scotland. The last friar there was Father Anthony Kelly who was recalled to Ireland by his provincial in the 1730s. The Irish Franciscans underwent a reform at the end of the nineteenth century. Several friars went to different places because of this, including two to Scotland. Father James (Clement) O'Neill, who had ministered in the Suir Valley for ten years since his ordination, went to the Diocese of Glasgow, spending seven years as a chaplain to the Franciscan nuns at Charlotte Street and another seven as parish priest of Saint John's, Stevenston. Father Patrick (Bernardine) McMullen also went to Glasgow Diocese in 1900, working first as a chaplain to the Little Sisters of the Poor, then replacing Father O'Neill at the Franciscan Nuns in Charlotte Street, and looking after the Franciscan teaching sisters at Bothwell from 1912 until his death in 1945.

Many Irish members of the English province, for example Father Noel O'Dwyer, ex-provincial and guardian in Glasgow, have worked in the Lowlands in the twentieth century. Irish friars fluent in Irish have been popular for parish missions in the Highlands and Islands. All things considered, the Irish Franciscans have played a major role in keeping Catholicism alive in Scotland.

Chapter 3

ESTABLISHING THE CHURCH IN NEWFOUNDLAND

It was Talamh an Éisc for many Irish seafarers who crossed the Atlantic each summer to fish the rich waters of the Grand Banks. Newfoundland was discovered and claimed for England by John Cabot in 1497, but occupied by the French from 1662 to 1713. The harbours of the south coast of Ireland were the last ports of call for boats from the English West Country on their way west. They often picked up – illegally – Irish crew. A small Irish colony had been established at Conception Bay even before the departure of the French in 1713. Many others followed and by 1763 one third of the population was Irish-speaking, suffering from neglect and semi-official persecution. Even today an Irish tradition underpins the way of life in Newfoundland.

The French had provided military chaplains for the Catholics on the island, among them some Franciscans from Paris. When they left, the Irish often travelled all the way back to Ireland to receive the sacraments. A number of Irish Augustinian priests worked in Newfoundland for a couple of years. In January 1784 three Waterford men applied to London for a priest to minister to them in Newfoundland. The British Government approved the request.

As a result of the hope which the Irish Franciscans felt during the 1780s they gave a positive reply to this request and opened their first foreign mission – to Newfoundland. Late in 1784 Father James Louis O'Donnell arrived as prefect apostolic. A native of Knocklofty, Co. Tipperary, he joined the Franciscans in Limerick, did his novitiate in Boulay, France, and studied in Rome before his ordination in 1764. Father O'Donnell then went to teach the Franciscan students in Prague. He served as Irish Minister Provincial from 1779 to 1782. After his arrival in Newfoundland other friars came to help him. The prefecture became a vicariate on 5 January 1796 and Father O'Donnell was consecrated bishop at Quebec on 2 September of that year. Due to the unusual circumstances, the ceremony was carried out by one bishop assisted by two priests rather than by three bishops. Bishop O'Donnell resigned in 1807 and returned to Ireland, where he died in 1811.

By 1800 the population of Newfoundland was 35,000 of which 27,000 (75 per cent) was Catholic. The island was divided into four regions for pastoral purposes but there were only six priests. The fish barons, part-time magistrates and other authorities made life difficult for Catholics. In 1790 a site for a church was refused because it might have encouraged the Irish to stay overnight. The government was also slow in paying O'Donnell a promised annual allowance of £75. The French Revolution caused further difficulties, e.g. looking after the spiritual needs of French prisoners-of-war, or having the holy oils captured by a French frigate in 1794. While on visitation in that year, the Bishop's ship was blown out to sea and drifted among icebergs for three days. His successor broke his ribs while climbing over a fallen tree on visitation in 1808. Father Patrick John Phelan was drowned while on parish visitation near Harbour Grace in 1799 – his ghost is reputed to walk the area still!

Bishop O'Donnell's successor was Patrick Lambert, who had been Irish Franciscan Provincial in 1803/4, and coadjutor bishop since 1806. He resigned in 1817 and was replaced by his nephew, Thomas Scallan, who had gone to Newfoundland in 1812. There were only seven priests on the island in 1817. Bishop Scallan went to Rome in 1823 to report on conditions in the area. He succeeded in getting more Irish friars to return with him, including Father Michael Anthony Fleming, who took over when Bishop Scallan died in 1830. As had happened with Bishop O'Donnell, only one bishop was at his episcopal ordination at Saint John's, with two priests assisting.

An energetic friar, Dr Fleming sought new missionaries in Ireland, both among his own Franciscans and the diocesan clergy. His first visit home enabled him to return with six priests to add to the three already on the island. He then ensured that the Catholic Emancipation Act of 1829 was applied in Newfoundland and also obtained relief for Dissenters and Wesleyans. There were then only five chapels in Newfoundland. By 1837 he could report that there were ten districts with ten good churches and twenty-two under construction, looked after by seventeen priests. While there had been no Catholic schools in 1830, there were now thirty-two. The Presentation Sisters arrived in 1833 and were joined by the Mercy Sisters in 1842. In 1841 Dr Fleming laid the foundation-stone of the cathedral and became first bishop of Saint John's when the vicariate was erected into a diocese in 1847. He also sent the first priest to work in Labrador. He was granted a coadjutor bishop in 1847 and later retired to a residence where he hoped to house a Franciscan community. The new cathedral was finished in time for him to say the first Mass there some months before his death in 1850. By then the anti-Catholic phase in Newfoundland's history was over.

Bishop Thomas Mullock, coadjutor since 1847, took over the diocese. A Limerick man who had studied in Spain, he had already proved himself a capable administrator before his appointment to Newfoundland. Since the episcopate of Bishop O'Donnell the ecclesiastical region of Newfoundland had included Labrador, Greenland and all areas up to the North Pole. In a series of moves Bishop Mullock persuaded Propaganda Fide to split up this vast area by creating a second diocese in Newfoundland (Harbour Grace, 1856) and combining most of Labrador and Greenland in one unit (Prefecture Apostolic of the North Pole, 1855). In 1855 he could report that about 50,000 of Newfoundland's population of 70,000 were Catholics, looked after by thirty priests.

Bishop Mullock opened a local seminary which he hoped would meet the need for future diocesan clergy. Before his death in 1869, Bishop Mullock had made it clear that he considered the time had arrived when the Irish Franciscans would no longer be needed on the island. At this stage there was only one religious among the thirty-three priests in Newfoundland.

Mullock's successor was the president of Clonliffe College in Dublin, Canon Thomas Power. An Italian Franciscan, Father Enrico Carfagnini de Scanno, Father Henry to his friends, who had lectured with the Irish Franciscans in Rome, had been brought to Newfoundland in 1855 to act as president of the new seminary. He moved into pastoral work as administrator of the cathedral parish of Harbour Grace in 1864 and became the second bishop of Harbour Grace in 1870. He did not get on very well with his clergy and there was general relief when he moved to the diocese of Gallipoli in Southern Italy in 1880.

Circumstances in Ireland never permitted more than a handful of Irish friars to go as missionaries – between two and five at any given time. The new local seminary led to a growth in local clergy. Irish Franciscan connections with Newfoundland ceased, for all practical purposes, in 1877, when Father P. A. Slattery, having previously resigned as president of the local seminary, returned to Europe. Another Irish friar volunteered to go to Newfoundland, but was not sent, and Father Slattery, who was proposed to succeed Bishop Carfagnini as bishop of Harbour Grace in 1880, was not appointed. A hundred years of Irish Franciscan work in Newfoundland had come to an end.

Chapter 4

PASTORAL EFFORTS IN THE USA

The first Catholics went to the the eastern coast of North America in 1634 under Lord Baltimore. They settled in Maryland, named after Henrietta Maria, the Catholic wife of Charles I. Although a Toleration Act was passed in 1649, discrimination continued against Catholics. The celebration of Mass was forbidden, Catholics could not hold public office and had to pay double tithes to support Protestant ministers. In spite of this persecution, Catholics did not refuse to fight in the War of Independence and were rewarded when the Constitution of 1787 abolished a religious test for holding public office. Freedom of religion was granted by the United States Congress.

The Catholics of America were deemed to be under the control of the Vicar Apostolic of London until 1784, when they were placed under Propaganda Fide in Rome. Father James Carroll SJ was named prefect apostolic. Five years later Baltimore became the first American diocese with Carroll as bishop. It was created an archdiocese in 1808 with the new dioceses of Bardstown, Boston/New York and Philadelphia under it. The Church's period of rapid expansion in America had begun.

Michael Egan was born in Limerick in 1761 and joined the Franciscans in Louvain, Belgium, in 1779. He studied in Prague and was ordained there in 1786. He later went to Rome to lecture at the Irish Franciscan College of Saint Isidore and was one of the friars who saved the College from extinction during the 1780s. He returned to Ireland in 1790 and served mainly in Ennis before his departure for the USA in 1803. He became pastor of Saint Mary's, Philadelphia. As the Church in America began to expand, Michael Egan was appointed first bishop of Philadelphia in 1808. He struggled valiantly against serious difficulties until his death in 1814.

Egan asked Rome to erect an independent province of the Order in the USA. This was agreed to in 1804 and he was appointed head of the new entity. In the event nothing came of it, probably because of the small number of friars in the northeast of the USA and across the border in Canada. At that time another Irish Franciscan, Father Patrick Lonergan, was working at Waynesburg, south of Pittsburgh, having come there from Sportsman's Hall. He had left Waterford to look after the Catholics in Southern Pennsylvania in 1796, and died in New Orleans in 1804. Farther north Father Henry Francis Fitzsimmons had accompanied Lord Selkirk's expedition from Scotland to Prince Edward Island in 1803, and then on to Glengarry. He withdrew to Newfoundland in 1812. Irish friars from that island also served in the USA or Canada for varying periods of time. Ambrose Fitzpatrick was in Prince Edward Island and New Brunswick before going to Boston in 1818. After Bishop Egan's death it was decided to appoint another Irish friar as head of the Order in the USA. Father Michael McCormick, who helped save Saint Isidore's College during the French occupation of Rome, was chosen in 1815, but remained in Italy.

Charles Maguire was born near Enniskillen in 1768 and received the name Bonaventure when he joined the Franciscans at Saint Anthony's College, Louvain. During his studies he became friendly with Father James McCormick, brother of Michael, and joined the pair at Saint Isidore's in

1793. He lectured in philosophy and theology until forced to flee to Gratz in Austria following the French invasion of Rome. By the time Napoleon had been defeated at Waterloo, Father Maguire had acquired a substantial income and was fluent in French, German and Italian. Several members of his family had emigrated to Pennsylvania in the USA and he decided to go there as a missionary. In addition to the normal faculties, he was empowered by the minister general 'to introduce our Holy Order into North America'. Towards the end of 1817 he arrived in Philadelphia but soon moved to the Pittsburgh area and took up residence at Sportman's Hall where Father Lonergan had worked. Without his knowledge he was proposed for the Diocese of Charlston by Father James Cowan, who had himself refused the honour.

In 1822 Father Maguire tried to establish a friary on a 113-acre site near Pittsburgh. At one end of the property he built a two-storey log house to accommodate a maximum of six friars and a log chapel. A cabin was erected at the other end for Poor Clare Sisters. Due to a lack of vocations the venture lasted only two years but it was the first Franciscan friary in North America since the time of the Spanish friars in California. Father Maguire continued to work in western Pennsylvania and was appointed vicar general of the area. He died there in 1833.

John Daly came from outside Athlone and received the name Benedict when he joined the Franciscans in 1828. In 1837 he presented himself to Bishop Fenwick of Boston and was given charge of the southern part of Vermont. The only priest in the area, he served twelve out-stations based in Castleton and Middlebury. He was strongly opposed by a Protestant element, and on one occasion the joists of the floor were partially sawn through, so that the chapel collapsed when the congregation arrived for Mass! In spite of many obstacles he established the Catholic faith in a large part of the present Diocese of Burlington. In 1854 Fr Daly retired to New York where he met the Italian Franciscans who had just arrived to found what eventually became the Province of the Immaculate Conception. He died in 1872.

These Italians also had an Irish connection. In 1854 Bishop Timon of Buffalo came to Rome for the Proclamation of the Dogma of the Immaculate Conception. He asked the Irish at Saint Isidore's College for friars for his diocese. They had no priests to spare, but an Italian Franciscan, Pamphilius of Magliano, who was lecturing in the College, responded, and agreed to lead a band of Italian friars to Allegheny. They arrived in June 1855 and progress was sufficient to erect the Custody of the Immaculate Conception in 1861. Later Franciscan history in the USA is complicated. Allegheny is now part of the Province of the Holy Name, one of eight provinces in the United States.

Another Irish Franciscan, Father P. J. Cuddihy, worked in the Diocese of Springfield, Massachusetts, from 1852 until his death in 1898. Many Irishmen have gone directly to the USA and joined the Franciscans there. Since the Second World War a number of the Irish Province – for example Leo Clifford, Aengus Quinlan, Timothy Quinlan, Richard Fennessey, Crispin Keating – have worked in the USA for extended periods, engaged mostly in specialised work such as the mass media, retreats or parish ministry. Their task has been different from the attempts of Irish friars to implant first the Church and then the Order in the United States.

Chapter 5

HELPING IN AUSTRALIA AND NEW ZEALAND

The history of the Catholic Church in Australia begins with the arrival of those tried after the Wexford Rebellion of 1798. A number of priests were sent into exile with them. After they returned to Ireland, it became necessary to organise a permanent ministry among the prisoners. An Irish friar, Father Richard Hayes, was in contact with his elder brother who had been living in Australia for seventeen years. Father Hayes petitioned Rome for priests in 1816, and a Cistercian, Father Jeremiah Flynn, was assigned to look after the estimated two thousand Catholics in Australia. The official attitude of opposition to the presence of Catholic clergy lessened and a number of priests, many of them English Benedictines, were recruited. Dom Edward Slater OSB was appointed vicar apostolic of an area stretching from the Cape of Good Hope across the Indian Ocean to Australia. This area was later divided and in 1834 Australia was set up as a diocese in its own right with John Bede Polding OSB as bishop. Within a few years an act was passed placing all religious groups in Australia on an equal footing and the Catholic population rose to about forty thousand.

During a trip to Europe in 1836, Father Ullathorne OSB, vicar general of Sydney, recruited a number of Irish priests, including two friars. Father Patrick (Bonaventure) Geoghegan OFM left Ireland in November 1838 and travelled to Australia with Father Ullathorne. Initially he worked in the Melbourne region, where he said the first Mass on Pentecost Sunday 1839.

Ten years later, when Melbourne became a diocese, he was appointed vicar general and undertook a successful recruiting trip to Europe in 1849-51. Many had expected that he would become bishop of Melbourne, but he had to wait another ten years until he was appointed the second bishop of Adelaide (1859-62). The new Diocese of Goulburn was erected in 1862. Geoghegan was appointed bishop there while he was back in Ireland trying to find more priests, but he became ill and died in Dun Laoghaire in 1864, before he could return to Australia.

The second Irish friar who volunteered for Australia in 1837 was another Dubliner, Father Nicholas Coffey. He arrived there in 1842 and soon became widely known as Dean Coffey. After some time in Sydney, he moved to Parramatta. In 1847 he joined Geoghegan in Melbourne. After another short stay in Sydney, in 1852 he returned to his beloved Parramatta where he remained until his death in 1857. A train with twenty-eight coaches was not sufficient to accommodate all those who wanted to attend his funeral!

The pattern of individual friars continued with Father Laurence (Bonaventure) Sheil, who arrived to work in Melbourne in 1853. He was president of and lectured in the local seminary until he moved to Ballarat in 1859. He was appointed Bishop of Adelaide in 1864, in succession to Dr Geoghegan. Dr Sheil made two trips to Europe, one in 1867/68 to recruit more priests and another in 1869-71 to attend the First Vatican Council. He was ill when he returned and he died in 1872.

Some Irish friars went to Australia for short periods. Three were from Cork: William Cunningham (Melbourne 1853-54), John Cronin (Melbourne and Hamilton 1853-58) and Thomas Barry (Melbourne 1859-62). Three who had been students together in Rome went to help Bishop Sheil: Charles Hugh Horan (Adelaide 1868-73; known as 'the Eloquent

Friar'), Patrick Keating (Adelaide 1869-70) and Patrick O'Keeffe (Goulburn 1870-82; Dean of Yass 1882 until his death in 1915).

Bishop Pompalier, initially Vicar Apostolic of Oceania, then Bishop of Auckland from 1848, asked the Franciscan minister general for help in 1859. Some Italian friars agreed to go to the New Zealand mission. They arrived in 1860 and were given a large area around Parnell. They had intended working through schools, but the Maori wars and the financial state of the diocese prevented this. Two Irish friars arrived to help them in 1867. Wenceslaus Francis McLoughlin became ill and had to withdraw to Australia, where he died. The other Irishman, James (Anthony) Mahoney, settled in. Bishop Pompalier retired back to France in 1868 and Bishop Croke, later Archbishop of Cashel, came to replace him in 1871. He found that seven of the sixteen priests in his diocese were Franciscan. He wanted the friars to become diocesan clergy and refused them a permanent foundation. As a result the Franciscans left Auckland in 1874. Mahoney went to California but returned after a few years to become vicar general of Auckland diocese in 1887 and died there in 1890. The friars returned to Auckland and were given a proper foundation in 1937.

So far individual Franciscans had gone to Australia. Bishop Sheil had hoped to establish a community in 1871, but died before he could bring this about. This was eventually achieved through the efforts of another friar who worked on his own in Australia for twenty years. Father Peter (Francis) O'Farrell was born in Co. Longford in 1809 and entered the Order with Laurence Sheil at Saint Isidore's, Rome, in 1832. He returned to Ireland in 1836 and was stationed in Athlone and Drogheda. O'Farrell became interested in the reform of Franciscan life, in particular by wearing the religious habit. He was appointed commissary visitator of the Irish Province in

1852 through the influence of Cardinal Cullen, and sought to promote his ideas on reform. He went to Australia in 1854 and worked mainly in the Diocese of Sydney. By saving up all his spare cash, he had nearly £4,000 available for a proper Franciscan foundation in Australia. Archbishop Vaughan of Sydney knew this and tried to persuade O'Farrell to take over two debt-ridden parishes. Father Peter's reply was direct: 'No friars, no money!' He retired to Ireland in 1874 and died early the following year.

Soon after O'Farrell's death, Roger Bede Vaughan, coadjutor bishop to the ageing Archbishop Polding of Sydney and very much aware of the money, invited the friars to make a foundation in the diocese. The Irish provincial definitory agreed in principle in 1876. Negotiations continued. Polding died in 1877 and Vaughan concluded a general agreement in January 1879 on the future Franciscan district – which just happened to include the two poor parishes refused by O'Farrell! The first three friars, Father Peter (James) Hanrahan, Father Martin (Augustine) Holohan and Brother Paschal McGinley, set sail in March 1879. The final agreement was not signed until 6 June 1879. Brother Paschal soon returned to Ireland, but three more priests arrived – Patrick (Fidelis) Kavanagh, John (Stanislaus) Joyce and Patrick (Leonard) Dunne. A problem then arose which was to bedevil the mission for thirty years: could five friars staff three parishes (Waverly, Edgecliff, Paddington) while forming one religious community? The community, based in Waverly, soon increased to six friars. From Waverly, they staffed two other residences with churches, at Paddington and Woolahara.

The number of friars in Australia increased very slowly due to a reform which was going on in Ireland. By 1908 there were only nine friars (including two on loan from the English Province), but the first Australian students were approaching ordination. Despite appeals for more missionaries it was not until after the First World War that friars arrived in greater numbers. In the interval disputes continued between the Archbishop of Sydney and the friars concerning the future of the Franciscan area, a large section of the south-eastern suburbs of the city. Eventually it was subdivided and large parts were taken away from the friars because they could not minister to the increasing population.

Permission had been granted for a novitiate in Australia in 1915 but it didn't materialise. Between 1916 and 1925 attempts were made to run a seraphic college at Rydal for boys interested in joining the Order. The Franciscan mission in Australia then consisted of the three original houses in Sydney and a house in Brisbane. In 1927 Father Fidelis Griffin was appointed commissary provincial and quickly established the framework for a Franciscan education system. A seraphic college with twelve students opened in January 1928 and had thirty-five students the following year. A novitiate opened in 1930 with five novices. A student house followed in 1932. It was no longer necessary for aspirants to undertake the long journey to Europe.

Father Fidelis suggested that the time had come to create an independent province. This required at least eight houses and was achieved with the opening of the friary in Auckland in 1937. The houses in Australia and New Zealand were erected into the Franciscan Province of the Holy Spirit on 31 October 1939. An Irishman, Father Andrew Wogan, was elected as the first Provincial. There were only 123 religious in the new province and the Second World War interrupted its growth. Nevertheless, the Province undertook a very successful mission in New Guinea in 1949. The first Australian-born Provincial, Father Joseph Gleeson, was elected in 1948. Some Irish friars remained in Australia until 1972.

Chapter 6

IN CENTRAL CHINA

Friar James of Ireland went with Blessed Odoric of Pordenone to China in 1316-20. Centuries later Maurice Connaughton from Ballinasloe joined the Franciscans in Killarney in 1906 and then went to Rome to study. Following a dispute with his superiors, he moved to the international Franciscan College in Rome with the intention of going to Japan. He happened to meet the Franciscan Bishop of Hankow, Gratian Gennaro, who persuaded him to serve in China. He was ordained in Hankow in 1913 and continued to work in that area.

At the Eucharistic Congress in Dublin in 1932 the delegate general for China, Father Gerard Lunter OFM, met Father Flannan O'Neill, the Irish Provincial, and discussed the possibility of an Irish Franciscan mission to China. Due to the great increase in vocations in Ireland, which it was feared would stretch the resources of the Irish friaries to their limit, the provincial had been thinking of a new mission, possibly in the Philippines. Attracted by the idea of China, he consulted Father Maurice Connaughton. On his recommendation it was agreed in March 1935 to accept an offer from Bishop Eugenio Massi, vicar apostolic of Hankow and an Italian Franciscan. The Irish would take over four administrative regions in the province of Hupeh. The area was about half the size of Munster with a population of four million. The main city was Suihsien, and the area included Yingshan and Anlu, which was the nearest city to Hankow.

Seven Irish friars arrived at Shanghai on 18 December 1935 where they were joined by Father Connaughton as head of the mission. They then went by boat to Hankow and by rail and bus to Anlu, which became the headquarters of the mission. This was seen as a temporary arrangement until a proper prefecture could be opened in Suihsien. The newly arrived friars studied Chinese under the guidance of a local teacher. They had their initial pastoral experience in the summer of 1936, and also had their first experience of the bandits who frequented the hilly parts of the mission. At the end of the year they were joined by three companions who were studying Chinese in Peking.

Early in 1937 the minister general agreed that the Irish section of the vicariate could become independent. On 17 June 1937 the Sacred Congregation of Propaganda Fide officially erected the new Prefecture Apostolic of Suihsien, with Monsignor Connaughton as prefect. He was officially installed at Anlu on 4 October 1937. At that time there were four Irish friars studying in Peking, one acting as procurator (in charge of supplies for the mission) in Hong Kong, and six (including the prefect) in the mission along with two Italian friars and two Chinese secular priests. A year later Monsignor Connaughton reported to Rome that missionaries were living at eight stations and serving thirty-five christianities (out-stations). A minor seminary was functioning at Anlu and work had begun on the construction of a residence for the prefect at Suihsien. The residence was never occupied due to the outbreak of war with Japan.

The Japanese had maintained a puppet state in Manchuria since 1931 and used the Marco Polo Bridge incident of July 1937 as an excuse to renew hostilities. As the war escalated, the Japanese advanced through the eastern end of the prefecture on their approach to Hankow. The friars set up three official and several unofficial refugee camps to cope with the thousands who fled in panic. The camps were open to people of any religion. Women, children, boys under fifteen, men over fifty-five and a small number of other men were admitted. The refugees were given two meals a day. The camp at Shiho became known as the 'Peaceful People's Town'. Anlu fell in October 1938 and the front stabilised a little to the east of Suihsien during the winter of 1938-9. Suihsien fell in the spring of 1939 and the situation remained unchanged for the next six years. One mission station, Liaochiatsai, which was in the Chinese controlled area, continued to function normally. Contact with Ireland was still possible.

Life continued more or less normally in the Japanese area. Five more Irish friars arrived and the first local friar was ordained. The refugee camps operated under the Irish tri-colour. Then the Japanese attacked Pearl Harbour and war became general. The Japanese froze bank accounts in February 1942 and in April arrested all missionaries, except those in Anlu. The prisoners were placed under house arrest in the Franciscan College at Chiaokow, outside Hankow. Three friars who had been in Peking were trapped in north China. Two of the Irish friars went to Shanghai in the hope of escaping from China. In February 1944 three of the friars from Chiaokow joined Monsignor Connaughton, two Irish friars and two Chinese priests in Anlu where they were confined to the mission compound for nearly a year. The restricted living conditions led to some psychiatric problems. An attempt to resume missionary activity early in 1945 was unsuccessful. Only after the end of the war in the Pacific in August 1945 could the missionaries return to their stations. The people were extremely glad to have their priests working among them again. The dedication of the friars in looking after refugees was rewarded with several conversions. The Chinese did not change religion easily, but once converted were extremely dedicated.

The conflict between Communists and Nationalists which

had been dormant during the fight against the Japanese re-emerged as a full-scale civil war late in 1945. The strain of the war years and house arrest had taken its toll, and several friars who were no longer fit for missionary duty had to return to Europe. In 1947 all the missions were functioning and a total of twelve priests, not all Irish, were active. In August, five new priests and five sisters of the Franciscan Missionaries of the Divine Motherhood arrived.

Communist forces began to infiltrate the northern end of the prefecture in August 1947. By Christmas everywhere except Anlu was under their control. A counter-offensive by the Nationalists expelled them in the spring of 1948, but the communists returned in the autumn. Given the experiences of foreign missionaries in other areas, the Irish friars were ordered to withdraw since it was anticipated that the Nationalists would return. The five remaining pre-war missionaries were sent home on holidays so that they would come back refreshed. Unfortunately American help for the Nationalists was withdrawn in the belief that such a move would force both sides to negotiate a peace. The result was a Communist victory.

On the instructions of the Franciscan delegate general most of the Irish friars fled, while the Chinese, one diocesan priest and three Franciscans, went underground. Monsignor Connaughton and a companion remained in Anlu to maintain a Catholic presence in the area but were placed under house arrest. Because of health problems they withdrew to join another friar in Hankow in the summer of 1950. The younger friar was diagnosed as seriously ill and received permission to go to Hong Kong in December. The authorities in Rome ordered Monsignor Connaughton to resign. He left Hankow on Good Friday 1951 and spent his remaining years in California where he died in 1967.

Father Dominic Ch'en OFM, who was appointed to

replace Monsignor Connaughton, was shot by Red Guards in Hankow, probably in 1970. His beatification is now under consideration. We know that another priest managed to live in the area for over forty years. One Irish Franciscan had remained in the Columban Procuration in Hankow. He was ordered to withdraw in December 1951 and took up a position lecturing in the Chinese seminary in Macao until 1954. Another Irish friar took charge of the Franciscan procuration in Hong Kong in 1950. This had been under Irish control from 1936 until 1939. He remained there until 1957, during which time its principal function was the reception of expelled missionaries. He then moved to Singapore, where he worked mainly among the expatriate Chinese community until 1969.

The Irish Franciscan mission in China had an unfortunate history. It was hardly established before it was caught up in a war situation. Despite the difficulties, the friars did their best and established the faith firmly in the area. Given the dedication of the Chinese Catholics, it is more than likely that an underground Church still exists. It has recently emerged that one of the old priests is still alive in the old Irish prefecture and has been given permission to re-open one of the mission churches. This is a sign of the real depth of faith implanted by the Irish.

Chapter 7

THE IRISH FRANCISCANS IN SOUTH AFRICA

The Irish Province had been unable to send out missionaries during the Second World War, although some friars served as military chaplains in Europe, North Africa and the Far East. By 1946 the Province had a number of volunteers eager to work as missionaries in distant lands. Two were sent to staff the College of Saint Albert in Cochin, India, in 1947, but difficult conditions forced them to return home. Five new missionaries went to China, but the mission there soon closed. The main Irish effort was directed towards South Africa.

An Irish Franciscan priest, Daniel Burke, had accompanied Patrick Raymond Griffith OP, first Vicar Apostolic of the Cape of Good Hope, to Africa. A native of Clare, Burke had joined the Franciscans in Wexford in 1809. He worked in Limerick, where he was superior from 1822 to 1828, and obtained the site of the present friary, and in Ennis, where he was superior from 1828 to 1830. He then went to Dublin where he became special advisor to Catherine McAuley, founder of the Sisters of Mercy. Griffith was consecrated bishop in Dublin in August 1837. With Burke and another Dominican, Griffith landed at Cape Town on Holy Saturday, 14 April 1838. Up to five priests had worked in and around the Cape prior to this, but the official church had now arrived. Burke travelled on to Grahamstown, where he took up the post of official chaplain with an annual stipend of £100. Unfortunately he died within a year of his arrival and was the first occupant of a graveyard which he had just purchased.

James Louis O'Donnell
Prefect Apostolic of Newfoundland
1784-96;
Vicar Apostolic 1796-1806; Titular
Bishop of Thyatira 1796-1811

Patrick Lambert
Vicar Apostolic of Newfoundland
1807-16; Titular Bishop of Chytri
1806-16

Thomas Scallan
Vicar Apostolic of Newfoundland
and Titular Bishop of Drago
1816-29

Michael Anthony Fleming
Vicar Apostolic of Newfoundland
and Titular Bishop of Carpasia
1829-47;
Bishop of Saint Johns 1847-50

Michael Egan
First Bishop of Philadelphia, USA,
1808-14

John Thomas Mullock
Titular Bishop of Taumaco
1847-50;
Bishop of Saint Johns 1850-69

The first Chapel, later Cathedral, at St John's, Newfoundland

Patrick Bonaventure
Geoghegan
Bishop of Adelaide 1859-64
Bishop of Goulbourn 1864-64

Patrick Bonaventure Sheil
Bishop of Adelaide 1866-72

Henry Hughes
Vicar Apostolic of Gibraltar
1839-45; Titular Bishop of
Hierapolis 1839-60

Peter Francis O'Farrell
1809-74
Regarded as the founder of
Franciscanism in Australia

Maurice Connaughton
Prefect Apostolic of Suihsein, China
1937-51

John Evangelist McBride
Vicar Apostolic of Kokstad and
Titular Bishop of Ezani 1949-51;
Bishop of Kokstad 1951-78

Wilfrid Napier
Bishop of Kokstad 1981-92;
Archbishop of Durban 1992

Liam Slattery
Bishop of Kokstad 1994

The first missionaries depart for China in 1935

The minor seminary in Anlu, China

The walls and moat around Anlu

Missionaries leave for Kokstad in 1949:
Frs Valerian Gavin, Kieran McCrann, Edward McSweeney and
Mathias McSweeney with Bishop McBride.

Palm Sunday procession, Garden of Gethsemane, 1942, with the Patriarch of Jerusalem in the centre. Fr Eugene Hoade OFM, Guardian of Gethsemane, is the friar at top right.

Saint Isidore's College, Rome, where most missionaries working in Central America, China, South Africa and Zimbabwe studied

The ruins of Bonamargy friary, County Antrim, the base for the Scotish Mission

Friars and Poor Clares celebrate in Harare, Zimbabwe.

The crib, Zimbabwean style!

A sanctuary in local style at Gandachibvuva, Zimbabwe

Church choir going strong at Murambinda, Zimbabwe

South African Franciscan novices and friars at Besters

A Catholic school for coloured children in Kokstad

Entrance to La Verna Retreat House, outside Johannesburg

The people meet after mass at Kokstad.

Athlone Friary Open Day for the missions, 1987

*Support for the missions: workers and friars with Bishops McBride
and Napier in Athlone, 1981*

Gerard Moore
Vicar Provincial in Central
America.

African couple ready for their
wedding in Harare,
Zimbabwe

Liam McDermott, first Franciscan Provincial in South Africa, with
John Hanley, OFM, Director of the Irish Franciscan Missionary Union

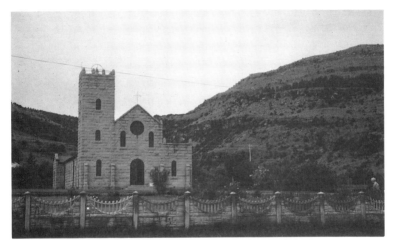

The church built by Germans at Matatiele, Kokstad, South Africa

The church that the Irish designed at Nharira, Zimbabwe

Saint John Vianney Seminary, Pretoria

The Griquas are descendants of the original Hottentot people of South Africa. In 1862 Adam Kok led two thousand Griquas into the area between the Drakensberg mountains and the Indian Ocean. He founded the town of Kokstad in 1869. The area had been under the care of the Catholic Vicariate of Natal, run by the Oblates of Mary Immaculate, since 1850. Bishop Charles Jolivet visited Kokstad in 1882 and found some Irish Catholic families, the menfolk being members of the Cape Mounted Rifles. He stationed a priest there and purchased a site for a church. The foundation stone of the Church of Saint Patrick was laid on 17 March 1884. By the turn of the century there were a hundred Catholics in Kokstad, most of whom were Irish. Then German Trappists arrived and opened a number of mission stations.

A new vicariate was split off from Natal and named Marianhill in 1921, with the Bavarian Adalbero Fleischer as bishop. He laid the foundation stone of the future cathedral in Kokstad in 1924. Soon there were about two thousand Catholics in the mission stations and four hundred in Kokstad. The Griquas had also begun to convert to Catholicism.

Bishop Fleischer of Marianhill invited Franciscans from his native Bavaria to help him in 1932. Their initial efforts were too dispersed and in 1935 they decided to concentrate on the area around Kokstad. This was erected into the Prefecture Apostolic of Mount Currie in 1935 with an ex-Chinese missionary, Father Sigebald Kurz OFM, as prefect. It was raised to a vicariate in 1939 and Father Kurz was consecrated bishop by Pius XII. The bishop and all except four of the missionaries were interned as enemy aliens during the Second World War. Bishop Kurz resigned in 1945.

The apostolic delegate to South Africa, Archbishop Martin Lucas, whose secretary was an Irish friar, Father Urban

O'Sullivan, invited the Irish Franciscans to take over. The first four missionaries, accompanied by the Minister Provincial, arrived in Kokstad on 27 December 1946. Three more came the following year. The Provincial, Father Evangelist McBride, decided to join them has Vicar Apostolic and was consecrated Bishop of Ezani on 25 July 1949. On 11 January 1951 Bishop McBride became head of the new Diocese of Kokstad with the erection of the hierarchy in South Africa.

There were about 4,500 Catholics out of a population of just under 400,000, mainly Xhosa, in Kokstad Diocese in 1951. It was staffed by twenty-three priests, thirteen Irish, nine German and an Austrian, and by six brothers, two Irish and four German. They were helped by seventy nuns, fifty catechists and eighty teachers in the eleven mission stations and seventy-six out-stations. Bishop McBride retired in 1978 and was replaced by Wilfrid Napier, first as apostolic administrator, then in 1980 as bishop. A native of the diocese, he had joined the Franciscans and studied in Ireland and Belgium before returning to Kokstad for his ordination in 1970. His episcopal ordination took place in Kokstad in January 1981 and he later became President of the South African Episcopal Conference.

The good work of the Irish Franciscans could be seen in the growth of the Church in Kokstad from 4,500 in 1951 to 45,000, out of a total population of 925,000 in 1980. The missions were staffed by eighteen Franciscans, forty-seven nuns and 127 catechists. A subtle change took place over the next ten years. The Franciscans in South Africa were reorganised and became a vice-province within the Order. Some of the Irish friars were replaced by others from England and South Africa. In a deliberate attempt to break away from an all-Franciscan context, the Comboni Missionaries took over an area within the diocese. Bishop Napier moved on to become

Archbishop of Durban in 1992 and was replaced by Liam Slattery, an Irish friar who had been a student with him in Ireland, in 1994.

Archbishop Lucas also invited the Irish Franciscans to staff a seminary for white clerics – this was before the Nationalist Party came to power in 1948 with their policy of racial segregation. Two Irish friars arrived and opened a temporary seminary at Queenstown, near Port Elizabeth, on 14 April 1948. The foundation stone of a permanent building was laid on 26 February 1950 in Pretoria, and the new seminary, dedicated to Saint John Vianney, opened on 1 March 1951. It developed rapidly and soon had a staff of twelve. In 1977 a decision was taken to desegregate the seminary despite its location in a white area. By 1980 there were sixty-five students, forty-seven of whom were residential. There were thirty white students, fifteen black, eleven coloured, three Indian and one Chinese. By 1984 the college was overcrowded, attempting to cater for seventy-five residential and twenty-two non-residential students. It was decided to move the faculty of philosophy to Hammanskrall in 1985. The theology faculty remained in Pretoria. The change in Franciscan structures in South Africa led to the handing over of control of the seminary to the hierarchy. A few Irish friars still teach there, but diocesan clergy are in charge.

The Vaal Triangle, the industrial heartland of South Africa, lies to the south of Johannesburg. There is a core population of whites in towns like Vanderbijlpark and Vereeniging. The main workforce lives in a series of black townships running eastwards from Soweto in the west, through Evaton, Boipatong, Bophelong and Sebokeng, to Sharpville. Bishop Hugh Boyle of Johannesburg, an Ulsterman, invited the Irish to take over some parishes in the Vaal Triangle. At that time he had ten diocesan and 110 religious priests looking after 135,000 Catholics.

35

The first Irish friars arrived in Johannesburg in 1955. Soon there were two friars in each of three parishes – Vanderbijlpark, Vereeniging and Barrage Farm. These were then mainly white centres but work soon began on the huge black townships which also came under the pastoral care of the Franciscans. Protest against the treatment of black people began at Sharpeville in March 1960. The police opened fire on the peaceful demonstrators. The late Father Columbanus Timmons OFM, pastor of the area, received a broken arm in the resulting troubles. For twenty years the Irish friars in the area were associated with the efforts to gain civil liberties for blacks. In the late 1960s one friar was expelled and a couple of others put under close police surveillance. More recently the friars have been involved in the case of the Sharpeville Six. They have also built up the church structures in the townships. Thirteen Irish priests and one brother were working in the Vaal Triangle and Boksburg in 1966. With the changes in Franciscan organisation, the Irish friars are still heavily involved in the townships as well as the parish at Vereeniging and La Verna Retreat Centre at Barrage Farm. The provincial house for the Order in South Africa was at Vanderbijlpark, a white parish, from 1985 to 1991.

The friars came to Boksburg near Johannesburg in 1957 to run a minor seminary. They later took over pastoral responsibility. In 1965 a new coloured township called Reiger Park was set up and a friar sent there to take pastoral charge. He set up a small library. In 1970 a nun joined him to take charge of education. A school and church were built and rapid expansion followed. The complex now provides medical facilities, an AIDS clinic, a day centre, a language laboratory and a computer centre. Over 5,000 students attend each year.

Originally the Irish friars in South Africa came under their own local superiors. In January 1959 the five houses of

Pretoria, Vanderbijlpark, Durban, Salisbury and Barrage Farm were erected into a commissariate with Father Urban O'Sullivan as Provincial Delegate. Rhodesia became an independent mission in 1966 and the commissariate was upgraded to a custody in 1968. Other Franciscan groups operating in South Africa included Bavarians in Kokstad and English friars in Ermelo and Volksrust. A number of South Africans came to Europe to enter the Order, but distance and expense caused the Franciscan authorities to discourage others from following. As fewer friars from Europe were interested in going to an increasingly troubled South Africa, the Franciscans there began to make their own arrangements. The Franciscan Federation of Southern Africa was erected in February 1977. A novitiate opened at Besters in 1980 followed by a student house at the Kraal outside Pretoria in 1980 and a pre-novitiate in 1982. A number of young local men joined the Order.

Under the Federation the friars in South Africa had remained members of their home provinces. The next step was complete amalgamation. The vice-province of Our Lady Queen of Peace in Southern Africa was erected on 12 April 1985 with eighty solemnly professed friars and ten in simple vows. Of these, forty, including the new provincial, Father Liam McDermott, were Irish. With integration, all members of the vice-province, be they English, Irish, Scottish, German or African (black, coloured or white) work together in unity, a wonderful example to the new multi-racial government of the country. The Irish still tend to work in the areas they know best – Kokstad and the Vaal Triangle. Three members of the vice-province (one African, one English, one Irish) are bishops, all in the province of Durban. While only three friars are still legally members of the Irish province, there are still bonds of friendship and appreciation between the friars in Ireland and those Irish men who have done so much to build up the Church in South Africa.

Chapter 8

THE IRISH FRANCISCANS IN ZIMBABWE

Zimbabwe was part of the Zambesi Mission given to the Jesuits in 1879. Starting in 1892, they opened mission farms to train people, hoping that they would become Catholics and form a base for expansion. The Mariannhill Missionaries, who worked through schools, arrived in 1902. The Prefecture of Salisbury was erected in 1927 and became a vicariate in 1932, with Matabeleland as the Prefecture of Bulawayo. The first bishop in Salisbury was Aston Chichester, an English Jesuit. He built up an African clergy and sought outside help. The Swiss Bethlehem Missionaries came in 1938 and took over the future Diocese of Gwelo. Bulawayo became a diocese in 1951. The Spanish Missionary Institute came in 1949 to the future Diocese of Wankie. Irish Carmelites arrived in 1946 to look after the future Diocese of Umtali. The hierarchy was established in 1955, when 142 priests with 353 nuns and sixty-five brothers cared for 114,000 Catholics. Archbishop Francis Markall SJ succeeded Archbishop Chichester when he retired in 1956. East German Jesuits arrived in 1959 to look after the future diocese of Chinhoya. Archbishop Markall retired in 1976 and was succeeded by an African, Patrick Chakaipa. There are now about 800,000 Catholics in Zimbabwe.

A pioneer column, which included five Dominican nuns and a Jesuit, entered the country in 1890 and raised the British flag at Fort Salisbury. The colony of Southern Rhodesia with Malawi existed from 1953 to 1964. Malawi and Zambia became independent with black majority governments. Rhodesia had a white minority government, which declared independence in 1965. The black majority organised political and armed opposition. As guerilla warfare spread, the Church was victimised by both parties. The Catholic bishops condemned violence, supported African demands for equality and preached against racial discrimination. Several priests and a bishop were deported. The black majority won and Zimbabwe gained its independence in 1980.

Archbishop Markall invited the Irish Franciscans to Rhodesia in 1957. The Provincial, Father Hubert Quin, sent Father Cornelius Heffernan as negotiator. He arrived in April 1958 and was joined by Father Samuel Hanley. On 4 July 1958 the friars signed a contract to take the parish of Waterfalls in Salisbury, and the country districts of Charter and Hartley.

Waterfalls was named after a waterfall where the Pioneer Column halted on the night of 11 September 1890 before founding Salisbury. A census in 1958 found 1300 Catholics from twenty-six nationalities. The most close-knit group were the Portuguese, with their traditional devotion to the Madonna, Fatima and processions. The Italians presented an outdoor statue of Saint Francis to Waterfalls Church in 1963. The English-speaking whites were tradespeople who came during the optimistic 1950s and moved on when times changed. The coloured people became the most active section of the parish. They opened Saint Anthony's Hall and Community Centre in 1971. The Africans were the poor of the area, either domestic servants or labourers. Initially confined to the townships of Harare and Highfield, they now dominate the parish. The Waterfalls friars insisted that the parish would be an integral unit with equal treatment for people of any race.

Fathers Cornelius and Samuel lived with the Jesuits until they got their new friary in March 1960. They said Mass in Lochinvar School and later at the TMB Hall. They got the present site in August 1958. In September 1959 they opened a little hall, which served as a temporary chapel. The first Mass in their new church was said in August 1960 and the formal opening by Archbishop Markall took place on 2 October 1960. The Secular Franciscan Order started in June 1961.

Father Kevin (Noel) Kinnane was general secretary to the Rhodesian Episcopal Conference from 1961 to 1976. There was an ecumenical gathering of Anglican and Catholic tertiaries at Waterfalls in October 1969, and two ministers general visited the friars there – Fathers Constantine Koser, in 1970, and John Vaughan, in 1985. The first out-station opened in 1971 at Saint Anthony's Hall, Ardbennie. Fifty thousand copies of the Peace Prayer of Saint Francis were distributed during the Franciscan Year in 1982. The number of families in the parish had risen to six hundred by 1985, and the first Zimbabwean Franciscan priest, Hilary Steblecki, was ordained in August of that year. A new presbytery was built for the parish friars and a nearby house purchased as the 'town house' for friars up from the country mission.

Fathers Boniface Gaynor and Jim O'Byrne came in May 1959 to work in Charter and Buhera. A contract for these areas was signed with the diocese on 8 September 1959. It was intended that this would be an independent jurisdiction or diocese staffed by Irish Franciscans. They picked Enkledorn – 'the single thornbush' – otherwise Chivu, or Our Lady of Lourdes Mission, as the base for their mission. The area was occupied by white Afrikaaner Dutch Reformed ranchers. Being church-goers, they wanted their staff to practise religion as well. The early ministry involved saying a monthly Mass in each compound where the blacks lived.

Enkledorn had been evangelised by Jesuits from Driefontein, who opened a school at Chivu in 1919. Catechumens walked to Dreifontein and spent a month there before baptism at Easter. They repeated this walk three times a year to receive Holy Communion. Father William Donovan took up residence on the Lancashire Estate in 1939 and worked in the area until 1958. Father John Gough replaced him until the friars came in 1961. They built a residence and church at Enkeldorn, which opened in 1963. With little prospect of adding to the thirteen Catholic schools in the area, the friars abandoned the 'school' concept of mission for a 'church' approach. They soon had twenty-five Mass centres in operation.

Mount Saint Mary Mission, Wedza, became the second Franciscan mission centre early in 1962. Wedza was founded by Mariannhill monks from Monte Cassino in 1924. Later on, African sisters of the Little Children of Our Blessed Lady opened a school. The Irish Little Company of Mary started a hospital and the friars had a temporary chapel ready by Holy Week 1962. From 1969, they encouraged a farmers' co-operative which has been a great success. Wedza was the residence of the religious superior of the mission for many years. Some thirteen Mass centres are served from there.

Wedza was the first Franciscan area affected by war. The mission was investigated by the authorities in October 1976 and the school was forced to close in 1977. Two friars and one sister working in Wedza were deported. Repeated military incursions forced a temporary evacuation in February 1978. The sisters kept the mission going and a priest said Mass there occasionally until the friars returned in March 1980. Work on a new church began in 1983 and it was blessed on Saint Patrick's Day, 1984. The Blue Nuns withdrew in 1991.

Gandachibvuva, 'that which overflows', i.e. the local waterfall, was one of the old mission centres served by the Jesuits from Driefontein. With a formed Catholic community and plenty of water from the nearby Mwerahari river, it was an attractive site for a residence. Father Schmitz opened a school at Dzikit's Kraal around 1920. Father Donovan was there from 1939 to 1945. The friars got a site in 1960 and named it after Saint Anthony of Padua. Initially served from Murambinda, a residence was opened in March 1963. Twenty-three Mass centres are served from Gandachibvuva. African sisters opened a school, social centre and clinic. Although the friars were officially expelled in February 1978, local leaders ensured that one remained until January 1979. Work on a proper church began when the missionaries returned in 1983 and it opened in June 1987.

On 4 June 1963 a new church was blessed at the fourth residential mission, Murambinda, or Saint Richard's Mission (in memory of young Father Richard Clancy OFM, who died in 1962). The friars built a small church and residence at Mombe in 1959. The availability of water and roads attracted them to Murambinda in June 1961. There were over twenty out-stations in 1965, later increasing to about fifty-six. The first sod for a hospital for the Blue Nuns was turned on 7 October 1965. The war forced Saint Richard's to close in May 1979 but it re-opened in June 1980, with a local priest, Father Alois Chinanga, in residence.

Nharira means the look-out post, a reminder that this centre, also know as Saint Francis of Assisi Mission, had a problem with cattle-raiding in the old days. Jesuits visited the area from 1910. Father William Donovan SJ ministered there from 1939 until 1958. The friars started work on a chapel early in 1964 and had moved in by the year's end. With help from the Beit Trust, they opened what became a mixed boarding-school in January 1965. The enthusiasm of the children for education ensures that there is no problem with discipline. Work on a new church began in 1969. The school and mission closed in February 1979 after the buildings were burned by guerrillas and government forces used it as an operational base. A friar returned in October 1980. The school re-opened in 1981 and now has 700 boarders, a third of them Catholic. It is run by trained locals, who are proud that they are one of the few schools with a complete second level.

In 1964 the friars discussed moving into Marandellas, which included the tribal trust area of Chiota, the black township of Dombotombo and the town of Marondera with a large school, Nagle House, run by the the Irish Presentation Sisters. This region came within the ambit of the Monte Cassino monks. The first resident priest was Father Charles Shackles SJ, who came in 1952 and obtained a forty-acre site for a church, residence, convent and college in 1954. Father Patrick Moloney SJ took over in 1957 and a proper church was opened and consecrated by Archbishop Markall on 23 October 1960. Father Soggie came in 1960 and was replaced by Father Thomas Warrington SJ in 1963.

The friars arrived in July 1966. The church sanctuary was updated in 1968. Two Sunday Masses were said in English and one in Shona. A local lad, Alois Chinanga, was ordained for the diocese in 1971 and helped in several of the Franciscan missions during the war years. One friar came to look after the Chiota and Muhusehua black districts in 1970. Marondera church and college were literally on the wrong side of the tracks for those living in the black township of Dombotombo. The friars opened a hall there, which also served for Mass, in 1987. The Kiltegan Fathers took responsibility for this side of the parish in 1992. Friars who died in Zimbabwe, Fathers Alphonsus Ryan and Frank O'Flynn, await the last trumpet at Marondera.

The friars opened a residential mission dedicated to Saint Brendan at Dorowa in 1969. Near a phospate mine, it was hoped that it would become a small town. Three African sisters came to help in 1973. While the sisters continued their work, the war situation forced the friars to abandon Dorowa in December 1978. They also discovered that their house, built on an anthill, was slipping into the local river. The mission is now served from Murambinda.

Monte Cassino started as a Marianhill mission in 1902. The Precious Blood Sisters came later. The English Jesuits took over in 1929, but handed over ownership to the sisters in 1970. Since it and the sisters' developments in Macheke were in Marandellas district, the friars took over pastoral responsibility and a friar was based at Macheke from 1972. Both missions closed in August 1978 because of war conditions. The area has been served from Marondera or by retired priests since then. Monte Cassino was the site of the first Custodial Chapter of the Zimbabwe Franciscans in 1992.

The mission in Rhodesia began under the Irish Minister Provincial. The foundation in Salisbury, with Pretoria, Vanderbijlpark, Durban and Barrage Farm in South Africa, were erected into a commissariate under Father Urban O'Sullivan on 1 January 1959. Father Cornelius Heffernan, as superior of the house in Salisbury, headed the mission in 1960. The increasing number of friars led to the Franciscan Area being split off as the Mission of Enkledorn, with Father Boniface Gaynor as religious superior, in 1963. The commissariate became the custody of Southern Africa in 1966. In practice Rhodesia became an independent mission with its own religious superior in 1969. The Rhodesian friars met in January 1976 and decided that Waterfalls friary and the Franciscan area should be one independent entity within the Franciscan Federation of Southern Africa. This became the

Vicariate of South Africa in 1985. Zimbabwe then returned to direct dependence on the Irish Province until its erection as the Custody of the Good Shepherd on 9 October 1990.

The original contract foresaw that the Franciscan area would become an independent jurisdiction. Doubts were expressed about whether it could become self-supporting. By June 1960, the friars were working in Buhera and Charter, with a promise to take on Gatooma and Hartley. These districts had a population of about 276,000, including 16,000 Catholics, spread over 11,200 square miles. In that month the visitator general, Father Roger Huser, suggested that Maradellas and Wedza would go better with Buhera and Charter than Gatooma and Hartley. A compact triangle the size of Munster would replace a long banana-shaped area. The provincial, Father Celsus O'Brien approved the swap during a visit in June 1961 and it was formally agreed in late autumn. A contract was signed on 1 January 1962 and approved by the Congregation of Propaganda Fide on 10 July 1963. The friars also debated whether to concentrate on primary or secondary education, opting for the latter at Wedza and Nharira in 1964.

The number of friars in Zimbabwe was never sufficient. There were twenty-two priests in 1969, falling to eighteen in 1970 and to thirteen friars and one African priest in 1974. During the independence war, the government would not allow new friars in and expelled others. Numbers have remained at about a dozen since independence. Two local friars have been ordained and more are in training.

The traditional mission in Rhodesia began with the erection of a house for a priest, followed by a chapel, a school, clinic or hospital. The Franciscans took over existing structures and developed their own, some opting for the sacramental approach by baptising as many as possible. Others explored the area of Christian communities by putting in place basic groups which could continue indefinitely with occasional visits by a priest. A key feature was the election of leaders by each community. These were trained in the faith and on how to nourish it in a small community. The firm commitment involved was much broader than that of the traditional catechist and created a core of excellent Christian leaders. Starting in the Franciscan area, it has spread to all parts of Zimbabwe.

In 1971 some 17,500 out of a population of 331,000 in the Franciscan area were Catholics. The following year the visitator general, Father Sylvester McGoldrick, talked to the friars and sensed that, because of financial instability, manpower problems and the political situation, a fixed structure like a diocese would not meet the real needs of the people. Newly consecrated Bishop Patrick Chakaipa made a short visit to the Franciscan area in May 1973 and praised their work in training Christian leaders. He was still thinking in terms of a future diocese, while the friars wished to give up some of their area. The contract was reviewed in the light of Vatican II and renewed at the end of 1974. Missionaries were now seen as helpers and co-workers of the local church, which would be Africanised. A codicil to this contract was approved in 1979, bringing it into line with new Church thinking. The Franciscan area was placed firmly within the diocesan administration and the concept of an independent jurisdiction was laid to rest.

The war of independence brought major problems. Friars in country areas were caught between both sides. Troops would raid a mission looking for subversives, and a few days later the guerrillas would come asking for medical or spiritual help. A few friars returned to Ireland to recover from the strain of living in a war situation. Since new priests were refused entry and others were expelled, the number of friars in Rhodesia fell to ten by January 1978. At one stage all the country missions except Enkledorn and Gandachibvuvu were closed. The most famous Franciscan victim of the war was the charismatic John Randal Bradburne. Born in 1921, he served in the British Army before coming to Rhodesia to help the weak and the poor. A man of music and jest, he became a mystic and joined the Secular Franciscan Order. He worked at the Mtemwa Leper Settlement and was killed near there on 5 September 1979. His cause for beatification has been introduced.

The Franciscans in Zimbabwe became aware of the need to implant the Order as well as the Church. A postulancy and novitiate had opened in 1976, but with limited success because of the war. Two young men studied in Europe. The outlook improved after independence. The novitiate re-opened at Marondera with three novices in 1983. It recently moved to Gandachibvuvu. A pre-novitiate was held at Marondera in 1984, leading to the opening of a postulancy at Nharira in 1986. The professed joined their South African confrères at the seminary in Pretoria. A Franciscan institute for philosophy and theology opened in Livingstone in 1988 to serve Franciscans, Conventuals and Capuchins in Malawi, Mozambique, Zambia and Zimbabwe. This has moved to a permanent campus in Lusaka. There were seventy-one students in 1991: twenty Capuchins, twenty-eight Conventuals and twenty-three Franciscans (four from Zimbabwe). The formation programme in Zimbabwe has had a high departure rate, basically because of the cultural differences between Africa and Europe. The friars are addressing the fundamental question of what it is to be a Franciscan in Zimbabwe. The signs are hopeful.

At Easter 1980, two weeks before Independence, Murambinda, Wedza, Enkledorn and Gandachibvuvu were open and contact had been re-established with Christian leaders in Buhera. The new prime minister, Robert Mugabe, visited Wedza in October 1980 and expressed his appreciation for the work of the friars. During 1979 the friars planned their pastoral initiatives in an independent Zimbabwe and the contract with the diocese was renewed in 1984.

There was a dream to enlarge the Franciscan family in Zimbabwe by bringing in the Second Order of Saint Francis. Spanish sisters arrived from Soria in February 1985 and stayed with their sisters in Macheke to experience African conditions. The friars gave them the friary in Waterfalls. The Poor Clares moved in on 1 November 1985. Their community is well established and the first African sisters have been professed.

The Custody of the Good Shepherd in Zimbabwe was canonically erected on 9 October 1990 with Father Walter Gallahue as custos. The first custodial chapter took place in April 1992. It decided that the priorities would be inculturation, the RCIA programme, work for justice and peace, youth ministry and healing. After examining the contract with the archdiocese, the friars opted for a new one which would indicate a more inculturated presence in Zimbabwe and incline towards a self-reliant Church with integration into local structures. The friars would give up territory and make the implanting the order their first priority in serving the local Church. Maintenance had absorbed too much of their energies at the expense of mission. This view was endorsed by the Irish Provincial Chapter of 1993. A new contract was negotiated with the archdiocese in 1993/94, agreeing that Marondera would be returned to the diocese in July 1994 and Wedza in December of that year. The Irish Kiltegans took over at Dombotombo township in June 1994.

The basic question for Catholics in Zimbabwe as we enter the next millennium is: what does it mean to be a Shona Catholic? Is it knowing some doctrines, christianising local traditions, or good liturgical experiences? The most exciting part of Catholicism is Sunday Mass, with drums, songs and dance before God. Should our relationship with the supreme being be one-to-one or a matter for our family or tribe? Death is still a tribal matter. The people live in a spiritual world close to their ancestors, who are buried near the village and must also travel if the family moves. They can be a moral people, for example they say that 'to be angry is to lose an argument'. They are a creative people who claim that 'God gets bored with copies ... he prefers the original'. The friars now face the challenge of marrying the Franciscan vision with the Shona lifestyle to produce a vibrant and meaningful Christianity.

Chapter 9

ASSISTING IN CHILE AND LATIN AMERICA

Soon after he became pope, John XXIII appealed for priests to look after the spiritually undernourished Catholic people of Latin America. During the 1950s zealous missionaries from various North American religious groups, backed by plenty of money, were making inroads in traditionally Catholic areas. Pope John felt that drastic action was needed. Initially this involved fresh missionaries in the field, but later encompassed a whole new Catholic lifestyle. This grew out of the Second Vatican Council and various regional meetings of bishops.

In the spirit of this appeal, and following a visit to Ireland by the Chilean Provincial, Father Javier MacMahon, seeking an Irish student master for Chile, an Irish Franciscan, Father Eamon Masterson, went there in 1964. He was not involved in formation, but acted for a while as national spiritual director of the Third Order and helped the friars in a large urban parish in Santiago. Following more requests, the minister provincial, Father Celsus O'Brien, went on a fact-finding tour of Chile and El Salvador in 1967. As a result, three more Irish friars joined Father Eamon in April 1968. Another friar arrived in 1971. They came to assist the Chilean friars rather than found an independent mission. A contract was drawn up under which the Irish agreed to look after three parishes for ten years.

It took time for the Irish to find their feet, since the Chileans had a rather different approach, both as religious and as priests, from the Irish. By 1970 they were settling into their parishes in Santiago, Rapel and Limache. Three Irish priests, one of whom was the parish priest, were working with a Chilean priest and two brothers in a parish of about 45,000 people in Santiago, the capital. They evolved a system whereby the sacraments were not just handed out, but given only after detailed instruction. Two Irish priests and a Chilean brother were ministering in the country parish of Rapel which had a population of 7,000. A Chilean priest and a brother who also lived there ran a small agricultural college. Two Irish priests and an aged Chilean priest served the urban-rural parish of Limache in the diocese of Valparaiso, where the church had been severely damaged by an earthquake.

Two more friars arrived in 1974/75. This enabled two friars to move out in 1975 and live in a wooden shack among the poor in a very deprived area. In the context of renewing the contract with the Chilean friars and considering what had already been achieved, the Irish decided to move out of Chile in 1977. One friar remained behind and continued working among the poor until he was expelled by the government in 1983.

A number of Irish friars became interested in ministering in Bolivia at the time that the Chilean mission closed. By 1979 three were working in La Paz, but two left when the mission was not granted official status. The third remained teaching in a seminary until 1988. A few individual friars worked in other parts of Latin America for a number of years.

Chapter 10

EL SALVADOR AND CENTRAL AMERICA

Central America originally had two Franciscan provinces but both were suppressed in 1922. Over the next fifty years six provinces sent missionaries to the region; the last to arrive were the Irish. Following contacts between the Archbishop of San Salvador and the Irish Franciscans it was agreed that the friars would take over the parish of Gotera in the Diocese of San Miguel.

The parish of San Francisco covered an area of 400 square miles in a rugged mountainous country district with dirt roads and many rivers, and had a Catholic population of 65,000. There were ten towns and fifty-two villages, of which seventeen could only be reached by horse or mule. There was a large army barracks beside the church. The first Irish friars arrived in 1968 and a community of four lived there for the next decade. By then civil unrest was spreading in the country and the local barracks became a centre from which the military tried to terrorise the inhabitants of a large area. The friars tried to form basic Christian communities as outlined in the Medellin documents. By the end of the 1970s there were 300 trained catechists/leaders and four vocations to the Franciscan Order.

The closure of the mission in Chile and the withdrawal of the friars from Bolivia made additional resources available for El Salvador. The friars agreed to take over the parish of Our Lady Queen of Peace, Soyapango. This was a huge area, the equivalent of three urban parishes. By the beginning of 1984 there were nine Irish priests and two deacons in El Salvador. The parish priest in Soyapango, Father Ronan Ó Huallacháin, died in 1985; he was so loved by the people that they insisted that he be buried in the Church of San Bartolo. They wrote on his memorial card: 'An Irishman with the heart of a Salvadorean'.

In 1974 the minister general had erected a federation of the various Franciscan missions in Central America. Following extensive consultation it was decided to join all the missions in these countries into the Vicariate of Our Lady of Guadalupe, with effect from 12 December 1983. This became a full province with the same title on 7 June 1987. While a number of Spanish and Italian missionaries opted to remain independent, the Irish entered into the new unit enthusiastically.

After the amalgamation, two Irish friars moved to a new area called El Carrizal. This was a mountainous region in the north of the country, so remote that it had been practically abandoned by the Church. Communications were difficult and in more peaceful times it would have been an ideal centre for prayer.

Following the Central American Provincial Chapter in 1990, the Irish friars continued their work in Gotera (one friar), Soyapango (three friars) and Carrizal (two friars). Others moved to new places. The Irish have also occupied high office in the new province: Father Gerard Moore has been Vicar Provincial since 1990 and Father Peter O'Neill, Provincial Definitor from 1987 to 1993. Currently eight Irishmen are members of the Province of Our Lady of Guadalupe. The Irish have played a significant part in answering the call of John XXIII to restore the faith in Latin America.

53

Chapter 11

MISSIONARY BISHOPS

The many Irish Franciscan missionary bishops are often forgotten. A mission begins with the arrival of a few priests who are later gathered into a prefecture under a prefect apostolic – a priest with the title of monsignor. Prefectures grow into vicariates under vicars apostolic – bishops appointed to titular sees. Eventually the hierarchy is erected. Vicariates become dioceses. Bishops change their titles to those of their dioceses.

Michael EGAN from Limerick joined the friars in Louvain and was ordained in Prague. He was guardian of Saint Isidore's in Rome from 1787 to 1790. He then returned to Ireland, serving as guardian in Ennis, Roscrea and Castlelyons. The Catholics of Lancaster in Pennsylvania, USA, invited him to come there. He arrived in 1802, moving to Philadelphia, where his brother lived, the following year. He tried and failed to implant the Order in the USA. Bishop Carroll of Baltimore, in arranging an extension of the hierarchy in 1806, recommended Egan as the first Bishop of Philadelphia. This was approved by Rome in 1808, but wars in Europe delayed Egan's episcopal ordination until 1810. His ministry was hindered by a small faction who wished to impose a system of trustees. Egan died in 1814 at the early age of fifty-three. It is said that he was found dead, lying on the floor, hands extended in the form of a cross, before a painting of Saint Francis.

Michael FLEMING had a Franciscan uncle, and he took the name Anthony in religion in his honour. From Carrick-on-Suir, he joined the friars in Wexford and worked with his uncle in Carrick for several years. There he met Bishop Scallan and agreed to go to Newfoundland in 1823. Four years later he was appointed coadjutor and ordained Bishop of Carpasia in Saint John's. With only three priests in Newfoundland, he recruited nine Irish priests. By 1837 he had ten parishes, ten churches, seventeen priests and the first convent of nuns. Rome considered erecting Newfoundland as a diocese within the province of Quebec but Fleming opposed this. Thus Saint John's became a diocese directly under Propaganda Fide in 1847. Fleming felt that he had done his best, had a coadjutor appointed and retired to a friary building which he had built for himself, where he died in 1850.

Patrick Bonaventure GEOGHEGAN was the first Franciscan in Australia and also the first friar bishop there. His roots were in Dublin. After he joined the Order, he studied in the Province of Algarve and was ordained in Lisbon. He returned to work in Dublin where he met the Vicar General of Sydney Diocese, Father Ullathorne, and agreed to return to Australia with him. Geoghegan initially worked around Melbourne, Geelong and Williamstown, and many were surprised he was not made first Bishop of Melbourne in 1848. Archbishop Polding of Sydney had not included Geoghegan's name on his list for Melbourne, but did seek him as an assistant bishop in 1854. There was little surprise when he was appointed second Bishop of Adelaide in 1858. Geoghegan sailed for Europe in 1862 to recruit priests, look after his health and visit friends. He missed a meeting of the Australian bishops who suggested that he be translated from Adelaide to the new Diocese of Goulburn. This was done in 1864, but Geoghegan never reached Goulburn. He remained in Ireland, extremely ill with cancer of the larynx, and died in Dun Laoghaire in 1864.

Henry HUGHES joined the Order in his native Wexford and studied in Spain. He became associated with Cork friary on his return to Ireland. He rushed to Rome in 1818 to take over the ailing college of Saint Isidore and remained there until 1824, first as superior and then as lecturer. He returned to Cork as guardian, a post he later filled in Wexford and Dublin. He was elected provincial in 1837. Unaware that he was being considered for a bishopric, he went to Rome in 1839 in an attempt to settle a dispute between the friars and the Bishop of Waterford. To his surprise, he was appointed Vicar Apostolic of Gibraltar and ordained Titular Bishop of Hierapolis after his arrival in Rome. Gibraltar had been under Spanish-speaking vicars, with Church property administered by the so-called Catholic junta or elders. Hughes' brief as first English-speaking vicar was to get the property back from the elders. The case was fought in the lawcourts, and Hughes was imprisoned by the junta for quite some time. One result of this was that he became a folk hero in England. A sign of his concern for people was a check for £100 which he sent from Gibraltar for famine relief in 1847. Exhausted by the legal struggle, which he eventually won on appeal in London, he resigned and spent the last years of his life in the Wexford friary until his death in 1860.

Patrick LAMBERT was appointed coadjutor to Bishop O'Donnell in Newfoundland in 1806 and was ordained Bishop of Chytri in 1806. A Wexford man, he joined the Irish friars in Italy and spent most of his early years in Rome, serving as guardian of Saint Isidore's College from 1783 to 1785. He worked mainly in Wexford after his return to Ireland. Interested in education, he started a school which became Saint Peter's College. When the minister provincial died in 1803, Lambert replaced him until elections took place in 1805. The new provincial declined an invitation to become coadjutor bishop to O'Donnell and Lambert accepted the offer. Despite bad health, he still managed to sail around the coast of Newfoundland on pastoral visitation. He died in Wexford in 1816 when he returned to Ireland for the ordination of his successor.

John Evangelist McBRIDE was from Leitrim and had attended the seraphic college at Multyfarnham before joining the friars in Killarney. He was ordained in Rome in 1927 and spent some time in Louvain before going to Dublin, where he became superior in 1939. Poverty was rife in the area and he arranged a daily distribution of 150 loaves of bread. He was Provincial from 1942 to 1949, during which period he saw the opening of the House of Irish Studies in Killiney, the return of the friars to Donegal, the emergence of Australia as an independent province within the Order, the reinforcement of the Chinese mission after the war and the opening of a mission in South Africa. German Franciscans had opened the prefecture of Mount Currie, South Africa, in 1935. They were interned during the Second World War and could not obtain priests from Germany afterwards. The Irish accepted an invitation to help. John Evangelist McBride became Vicar Apostolic of Kokstad and was ordained Titular Bishop of Ezani in 1949, becoming Bishop of Kokstad when the hierarchy was erected in South Africa in 1951. Bishop McBride retired to Ireland in 1978, leaving a flourishing diocese in Kokstad, and died in Dublin in 1991.

John Thomas MULLOCK from Limerick joined the Irish Franciscans in Spain and completed his studies in Rome. As a young friar he found a proper site for Ennis friary and became a trusted administrator. He was in Rome on delicate Franciscan business in 1847 when he was appointed coadjutor in Newfoundland. Ordained Bishop of Taumaco before leaving Rome, he became Bishop of Saint John's when Bishop Fleming died in 1850. By 1855 he could report that there were 50,000 Catholics living in sixteen parishes staffed by thirty priests. A seminary had opened and there were eight convents of nuns. The following year Rome reorganised the area. Saint John's remained a diocese under Mullock and Harbour Grace became a diocese. Labrador, Greenland and related areas became the Prefecture of the North Pole, with the prefect resident in Greenland. Bishop Mullock, the last Irish Franciscan bishop in Newfoundland, died in 1869.

Wilfrid NAPIER became the second Bishop of Kokstad in 1981. A native of the diocese, he came to Europe to join the Irish Franciscans in 1960 and studied in Galway and Louvain. He was ordained in Kokstad in 1970 and ministered in the diocese. Named Apostolic Administrator of Kokstad in 1978, he was appointed bishop in 1981 and became an extremely active member of the South African Bishops' Conference, representing them at all the Synods of Bishops in Rome. With such an excellent background, he was translated to become Archbishop of Durban in 1992.

James Louis O'DONNELL from outside Clonmel joined the friars, studied on the Continent and served as chaplain to some noble families, before returning to Ireland in 1768. He was Irish Minister Provincial from 1779 to 1782. He then went to Waterford before leaving for Newfoundland in 1784 to take up the post of Prefect Apostolic and begin the task of building up Church structures. He divided Newfoundland into four areas, each with its own priest. Following a petition to Rome by the locals, Newfoundland was raised to a vicariate and O'Donnell ordained to the titular see of Thyatira in 1796. In 1805, worn down by looking after the spiritual needs of about thirty thousand Catholics, he applied for a coadjutor. When the new bishop arrived, O'Donnell retired to Waterford, where he died in 1811.

Thomas SCALLAN was a nephew of Bishop Lambert. Under his uncle's influence he had joined the friars in Italy and later worked with him in the Franciscan Academy in Wexford. He first came to Newfoundland in 1811, but returned to Ireland in 1814. He agreed to become coadjutor to his uncle and was ordained Bishop of Drago in Wexford in 1816. His first priority was obtaining more priests for the island. Ill-health dogged his efforts and he applied for a coadjutor during a visit to Rome. Scallan died in Saint John's in 1829, seven months after ordaining his successor.

Lawrence Bonaventure SHEIL succeeded his fellow friar Geoghegan in Adelaide in 1866. From Wexford, he joined the Irish friars in Rome and remained at Saint Isidore's as lecturer and master of students after his ordination in 1836. He returned to Ireland in 1839 and served in Cork for five years before becoming guardian in Carrick-on-Suir and Cork. He met Bishop Goold of Melbourne during a recruiting trip in 1852 and returned with him to Australia, where Sheil made a great impression. He lived in the bishop's house and lectured at Saint Patrick's Seminary. He was president of the seminary from 1853 to 1855, when he became Archdeacon of Ballarat. He then tried but failed to have the Franciscan Order officially introduced in the country. When the Australian bishops suggested Geoghegan for Goulburn in 1862, they included Sheil's name on their list for Adelaide. Thus he became the third Bishop of Adelaide in 1865. He was in Europe recruiting priests in 1867/68 and again to attend the First Vatican Council in 1869/71. He was not in good health on his return and died in 1872.

Liam SLATTERY was born in Portlaoise and grew up in South Tipperary, joining the friars in 1962. He studied in Galway and Rome before his ordination in 1970. After a short while in Ireland, he went to South Africa and spent five years working in the black townships around Johannesburg. He became Novice Master of the new multiracial Franciscan

Novitiate at Besters before going to teach at the national seminary in Pretoria. After six years as President of the seminary from 1985 to 1991, he returned to the novitiate at Besters, from where he was called to become the third Bishop of Kokstad in 1993.

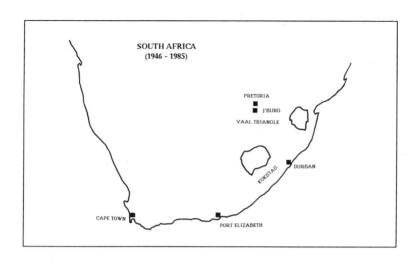

SOUTH AFRICA
(1946 - 1985)

PRETORIA
J'BURG
VAAL TRIANGLE

KOKSTAD
DURBAN

CAPE TOWN
PORT ELIZABETH

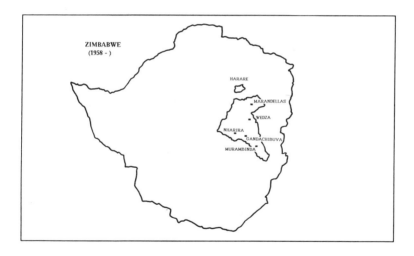

ZIMBABWE
(1958 -)

HARARE

MARANDELLAS
WEDZA

NHARIRA
GANDACHIBUVA
MURAMBINDA

61

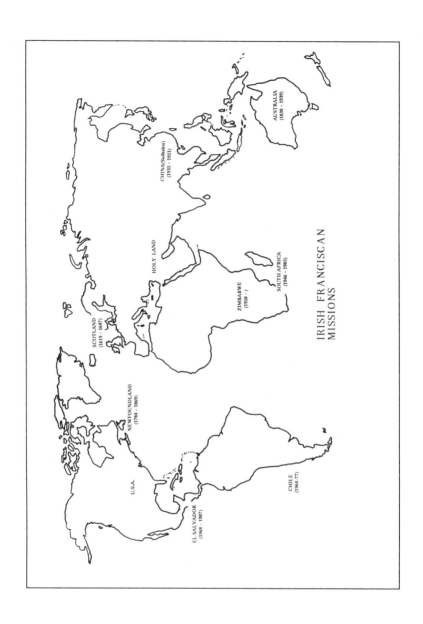

IRISH FRANCISCAN MISSIONS

AUSTRALIA
(1838 - 1939)

CHINA (Suihsien)
(1935 - 1951)

HOLY LAND

SOUTH AFRICA
(1946 - 1985)

ZIMBABWE
(1958 -)

SCOTLAND
(1619 - 1647)

NEWFOUNDLAND
(1784 - 1869)

U.S.A.

EL SALVADOR
(1968 - 1987)

CHILE
(1964 -77)

62

Ancient Seal of the very Reverend Guardian of Holy Mount Zion,
Apostolic Commissary of the Holy Land and Orient

Original Seal of the
Franciscan Province
of Ireland

Present Seal of the Guardian
of Holy Mount Zion